Make Irresistible Presentations: You Won't Have to Sell Only Help Them Buy

Category: Business & Economics

Author: Bob Oros

Publisher: Bob Oros Publishing

ISBN: 978-1-387-20022-1

Copyright 2017

Description: Your presentation may be focused on the wrong thing mainly because you are under the assumption that to sell you have to find the needs of your customer and then work up a presentation that will demonstrate how you can help fill those needs. Here is the problem with finding needs; we are looking for something that does not exist. No one really needs anything. Learn why people really buy.

Key words: manufacturing sales training, wholesale sales training, distributor sales training, food service sales, sales coaching, sales techniques, motivating sales people, job in sales, sales manager training, sales course, manufacturing sales training, online sales training, food sales jobs,

1. How to make your presentations irresistible

Your presentation is focused on the wrong thing mainly because you are under the assumption that to sell you have to find the needs of your customer and then work up a presentation that will demonstrate how you can help fill those needs.

Here is the problem with finding needs; we are looking for something that does not exist. No one really needs anything. I am sure you have everything you need to get by, just as your customers do. As a matter of fact if you took away twenty five percent of your competition, effective next Monday morning, how long would it take to fill the needs of their customers? Not long, probably a couple of weeks. It would be an exciting couple of weeks if we call on customers and asked them if they need anything and they actually said yes!

If you are not looking for needs, what are you looking for? Talking about what you need is really not very exciting. If you stop for a moment and ask yourself what you think about nearly every minute of the day you will find that it is the same thing everybody thinks about. You think about what you want. You think about your future! To get people excited about buying you must go beyond the need and find out what they want. What is in their future that, with the help of your products and services, you can show them how to get it?

You and I, and every person we know, LIVE IN A TOMORROW! That TOMORROW may be a few hours off. It may be this afternoon or next week, a month, a year, or even ten years from now. Ninety percent of the excitement in the PRESENT is the imaginary picture we are constantly recreating in our minds of a TOMORROW.

Every waking hour the mind of your customer glides out of the present into the future, and they see themselves as they will be tomorrow.

Everyone in sales has been searching for a key which would magically unlock the door of the mind of every prospect you call on. A key which will open a new world for us in the minds of every man and woman with whom we associate. Here it is, if you can hold it firmly and use it!

Ninety percent of the excitement in the present is the imaginary picture of the future you are constantly recreating in your mind.

It will always be a better tomorrow. We picture ourselves as happier then. We will be healthier, more comfortable, with less worries, with more leisure, with more money, with greater power ... we will strangely be freed of the realities that make today far from satisfactory. There will be no north wind, no drizzling rain! Only blue skies.

This attitude forms the texture of desire. It is at the base of the mind of every person who has lived in America for more than twenty four hours. It is our national philosophy, our habitual trend of thought. We know we are going to be better off tomorrow than we are today. Every waking hour our mind glides out of the present into the future, and we see ourselves as we will be tomorrow.

The business owner never likes the profit and loss statement of today... but tomorrow profits are going to climb! He or she pictures a new line of merchandise moving quickly at a greater profit.

Tomorrow the young husband pictures himself in his imagination as free from worry as to the economic future of his wife and children - then his insurance and retirement will be paid and provide for the necessities, his house will be paid, his automobile will be paid, his credit cards will be paid.

Today the manager must work three nights a week to keep his or her desk clean, but they picture a tomorrow when this new computer will clean the desk at five o'clock, unfatigued and with peace of mind.

Tomorrow! We live most of it today. It is so much better than today. The person who sits across from you now is not thinking about themselves as they are now - they are building a mental picture of themselves as they will be tomorrow and tomorrow and tomorrow... with this or that added, which they are about to purchase... which, when acquired, will make them much happier. They see themselves with more customers, with larger gross profits, lower labor costs and less taxes to pay.

How can the benefits of my products and services enhance my clients future? When we begin to think in these terms we have crossed the bridge from sales person to a true "Sales Consultant."

Once we begin to think in these terms, our prospects turn into customers and our customers turn into clients. We have set ourselves apart from the average "peddler" who merely has a sales pitch, and put ourselves in the position of a partner who is working for the same goals and objectives as our client. They will know that you "understand where they are coming from". They will know that you understand their problems and have an `insight' into what they are trying to accomplish. Once we can put them on the "magic carpet" and take them to a place where their future becomes a possible reality, you won't have to sell, you will only have to help them buy!

This is the secret of a sales. Your average sales person talks about the price, the competition or the product, always in the present tense. The professional sales person looks at their product or service from a different view point. The first question you ask when putting together your sales strategy is: What does my prospect or customer want? What are the pictures they have of their future? What are their goals? Where do they want to be next year, the year after, and five years from now?

I know you understand this. Most people don't. Take this secret and start creating pictures of success for your customer. Show them how much profit they are going to make using your products and services. Help them create a better future. Don't be a purveyor of bad news, be a purveyor of prosperity.

Comments:

In summation, the question we should be asking the customer is "how can I make your life easier? What issues or problems can my company and I address in your business to give you more free time, more profit, more piece of mind? "

Showing the customer that we think the same way he does, deal with the same daily issues and regularly step beyond them to provide solutions for our clients to "a better day tomorrow" through our expertise, commitment to quality and above all our dedication to serving them will help forge a strong and lasting relationship, profitable to both of us.

Chris Chase

The presentation should be based on the features and benefits of our service. Most of our clients focus on the "tomorrow", and we as sales people should do the same. After all, that is what we plan everyday for, right? It is our job to show how our service or product can enhance their "future". Find out goals your customers have, where do they see themselves in a year? These types of questions only make it easier to focus on the features or benefits we provide that will help the customer to reach future goals! That is what interest the customer, the FUTURE!!

Brooke Knight

Life is about making mistakes and learning from those mistakes. Taking what we learned and putting it to use in hopes of avoiding doing it again in the future. Study the company you want to sell to and try to figure out what will help them be successful and keep them ahead of the competition. Put your presentation together to show the business how they can continuously grow towards a successful future. Every business needs a map of where there are going or headed. Without it they get lost.

David Bradley

Bad presentations are based on what we think the client needs, because that is what we are selling. A good presentation will give a brief overview of what we are capable of doing followed by questions of what would help them run their business more effectively. They may say they have no needs, but we need to continue to talk and ask questions because they might reveal a need they may not realize they have.

Brandon Sanchez

This is correct. I am also a tomorrow person. I think about the future more than I think about today. I want to be on top in the future and I also want my client to be there as well. I think every proposal for new business has to have an element of future goals for my business and the fact that I want to be in the future of goals of my clients business.

Kathie Luttrell

Also, as much as we fanaticize about tomorrow, we love instant gratification. So selling on the immediate benefits as well as what our future golas are would be a powerful.

Morgan Frazier

We, as sales people, cannot rely on what business owners need. Their needs are a very small component of their business. For the most part their needs are met, that's why they are operational. Now they want to focus on tomorrow. People as a mass want to live for tomorrow because tomorrow is forever coming, while today will be gone shortly. Tomorrow has endless possibilities, and it's our job to help them see their "tomorrow." When your prospects know that you share in their aspirations, they'll no longer be just prospects.

Matthew Thacker

Sometimes we wish we had a crystal ball to help us see what is coming to us. The good thing is that we all have a crystal ball, but we just don't know how to use it well. A crystal ball is nothing but taking a look at existing information and asking key questions about it. When you get to understand that information you will predict the future. I think that the same thing happens in the selling business. You study your prospect and his business, original needs, how they bought before and past decisions made and the results obtained. That past information you have gathered may have pain but that is where experience comes from, mistakes. The past will help your understand the best way to communicate your ability to help in the future.

Yessie Narvaez

2. What percent of sales people fail due to lack of planning?

Seventy-eight percent of all sales people fail because they lack what skill? When asking that question to a group of sales people the answers are all over the board. Closing usually comes out as number one, objections are number two, after that it's a toss up between making presentations, getting people's attention, follow up and asking questions. The reason 78% of all sales people fail, or fail to reach their sales objective is due to a lack of planning. At first this may seem a little off balance, however when we take a look at what planning really is, it takes on a new meaning.

For example, let's take a look at closing. The best time to think about your close is when you are planning the call. Instead of taking in one product to show your customer, take in three different quality levels. Instead of asking if they want to buy your product or not, you can now ask them which product would best fit their needs. That is the choice close at its best.

Objections are another example. If we wait until we are in the buyer's office and he or she says "your price is out of line" it's a little late to start figuring out what to say. We all know the objections we run into, and again, the best time to overcome them is when we are planning the call.

Let's take a look at making the presentation. There are very few products on the market today that cannot be duplicated, turning them into a commodity. Why should a buyer switch to your product when the features and benefits are the same? Once again the time to find the "points of difference" that will make a professional presentation is during your planning stages.

How about getting the buyer's attention? The average buyer is interrupted every eight minutes. If they have been buying for any length of time they have "heard it all." What are you going to do or say during the first 60 seconds that will make the buyer lean forward and say "tell me more." If you are trying to think of something while waiting your turn to see the buyer, well, you get the point.

The old days of "hitting the street and making some calls" are pretty much in the past. Twenty years ago there was believed to be such a thing as a "Born Sales Person". Today we have to sell with "Surgical precision."

I am sure you would not like to have open heart surgery by a "born doctor" who understands the concept of open heart surgery but does not take the time to plan every detail of the procedure?

How would you feel about getting on an airline flight with a "born pilot" who understood the theory of flight but never took the time to file a flight plan.

How would you feel about eating in a restaurant run by a "born cook" who never had any training in food safety and never took the time to follow up on the cleaning details.

What about investing with a broker who "had a feeling" for the market and bought and sold without a detailed plan.

Most importantly, when you are buying something, how do you feel about buying from sales people who take up an hour of your time without having a well-prepared plan and presentation for the appointment. These unprepared appointments are usually justified as having "advertising value," or building a "relationship." However, today's profit and loss statements are viewed from the "Bottom line up." The bottom line of selling is to measure your call results with your call expectations. And call expectations are "planned" in advance.

The difference between an average sales person and a "Cutting-edge" sales professional is many times only a small difference. If a certain sales person is selling twice as much as another sales person, it does not mean the one producing more results is twice as good as the other. The difference may be only a few minor things that may even seem insignificant.

To keep your selling skills on "the cutting-edge" take the advice of a master salesperson, Abraham Lincoln. He once said "If I had six hours to cut down a tree, I would spend four hours sharpening my ax."

The bottom line of planning; spend at least four hours on a Friday Afternoon or Saturday morning going through each call you are going to make next week.

Comments:

Schedule planning time for your next week at the end of the current one; allowing nothing but dire emergencies to get in the way. You must make sure phone and email messages reflect the certainty of you unavailability. Once customers recognize that you are consistently engaged at that time, they will learn to make known their "emergencies" earlier in the day.

Jim Roth

Planning your day also makes you feel better at the end of the day, keeps your stress level down and keeps your attitude and focus at a higher level. In short, it makes you more efficient at your job.

Crocker Smith

I have definitely learned that planning my day and week makes me more productive. If I don't have a plan the "daily crisis'" suck me in and I never get a chance to leave the office. Planning helps me to stay on track with follow-ups. For me it easy to forget to check on clients or prospects if I don't have a visual reminder. I have a hundred things going in my head all day, planning keeps me productive and focused.

Brooke Knight

As I read this lesson, I thought of our sales-person, Heidi. Every day when she comes in to work, she spends the morning planning, then goes out in the afternoon. She plans out where she is going, the clients she will see, the supplies she needs to bring, and she also researches the companies. Now, if Heidi went directly out into the field without doing that, she could spend 5 or 6 hours driving around aimlessly, and stopping all over creation. The few hours spent planning, then executing it in the afternoon makes for a much more productive day, in less time!

Laura J. Czajka

3. What is the one skill that will make you a consultant?

What is the one thing eighty percent of all buyers dislike about sales people. The answer is not surprising: we talk too much. One of the most difficult things for many sales people to do is listen to their customers. The reason we talk too much is understandable. We called on the customer and asked for some of their time. This sets up a professional expectation on the part of the buyer. "You asked for my time, now tell me why you want it."

The pressure then falls on the sales person to deliver a presentation. This is the point in the selling process that separates the amateur from the professional. The amateur mistakenly believes that selling and talking are the same thing. The professional knows that you cannot sell anything until you first know what the customer wants. How can this be accomplished?

Instead of starting off the meeting talking about our products, services or company, start off by asking a few questions. "I am here to talk about how some of our services might be of benefit, however, before I start do you mind if I ask a few questions?"

What are the best questions to ask? One thing about our customers that we all agree on is that they have long memories. Ten years ago someone from your company may have made a mistake with this customer. It could have been anything from not receiving a credit to a phone call not being returned. If you are going to talk about a new product there may have been something about the broker or supplier that previously upset the customer.

The initial questions should always try to uncover any over riding objection the prospect or customer might have. Until we clear this objection away, our presentation, no matter how good or convincing it is, will fall on deaf ears.

Many times it is necessary to make more than one call on a prospect before they are ready to by or before we qualify them as someone who would be profitable for us to work with. The initial call should always start by gaining information.

Many sales presentations are designed to go through the entire presentation before handling the objections that are sure to arise. Once again any objections your potential customer has for not giving you an order should be handled first. The reason is simple: If there is some obstacle that seems insurmountable, your prospect will not hear anything else you have to say until you deal with it.

In the back of the prospects mind, maybe not even consciously, they will be thinking that whatever you say doesn't really count, because there is an overriding reason they cannot give you the business anyway. As long as an obstacle blocks your path, you will never get past it until you bring it out in the open and deal with it. The only way you can bring this obstacle out in to the open so you can deal with it is by asking questions.

Our second group of questions should focus on what our customer or prospect is trying to accomplish. Are they trying to lower food cost, lower labor cost, increase quality, increase check size, increase customer count, etc.?

Finally, after we remove any objections or problem that may be on the table, and after we have a clear understanding of where our customer or prospect is going, we are in a position to make our presentation.

Asking questions rather than talking and making positive statements puts us in the category of a consultant. The true purpose of a consultative sales person is to find out what your customer wants and help them get it. To accomplish this we have to listen more that we talk.

Here are two good quotations for the dashboard to help remind us to listen more than we talk:

"It is better to be silent and thought a fool, than to speak and remove all doubt."

"Whoever talks the most during a sales presentation ends up with the product."

The bottom line: simply encourage your customer to talk- and to keep on talking,-- ask carefully thought out questions and listen. If you can get them to talk enough, they simply cannot disguise their real feelings or real motives.

Comments:

You know it's funny, it is easy to get caught telling the company's story. I get on my soap box and just cut loose. I rant and rave and about quality and service and how I'm going to solve all their problems. I have even spent 30 minutes telling my story only to find out they buy enough of what I sell to matter. It is much harder to simply ask them about their business and get to know them. Lately I have been scheduling appointments in order to do just that, "find out about your business".

Dave Ferren

Time management, setting a specific amount of time from your perspective for the presentation, and a list of questions designed to keep the customer imparting the information you need to address his issues are both good ideas for a call.

If I go into a presentation open-ended I find myself dragging it out and having to talk to fill time. With a specific time plot and a list of questions there is a stopping point where you take the answers I have received and move on to setting up the next visit and "solving" them.

Also, knowing who you are talking to helps. I gave a fantastic presentation to a manager recently. He was attentive as I described the company I work for and the services we provided. He answered all the questions I asked with candor and appeared enthusiastic about the opportunity to do business with me. It was only AFTER I gave one of the best opening pitches I had EVER given that I found out I was talking to the wrong person!

Chris Chase

I learned this lesson from my dear wife, and yes even after 30+ years with her, about the same time I have been in sales I'm still working to do more listening and less talking on my part.   How many time does your wife just needs you to listen to her, not you talking on how you're going to fix it.

David Vize

Listening is the best way to find out what the customer wants as well as make him feel that you are interested in his business. Everyone likes an audience. I have seen sales reps (and Managers) who feel like it's all about them. It's not. It's about the customer.

Larry Edmondson

Please repeat after me...

"I am not selling something to somebody- I am solving issues that are plaguing my clients". "I make a difference in someone's life everyday". This is what separates the tares from the wheat- I mean the salesman form the consultant. Preparation is the key. You will need two key items

1) a list of OPEN ended questions and

2) an OPEN mind (no preconceived thoughts). Do you really know what your client wants & needs OR do you just think you do????? Remember: Stop- Ask- Listen. Repeat.

OK- I have a revolutionary idea. Are you ready? Listen carefully and take notes. Here is pen and paper, write it down (hand pen and paper to person). What we are going to talk about now WILL affect the rest of your life. Listen carefully. Here we go!

If you ask these five questions, everything your client needs will fall out on the table in front of you.

WHAT: What is the biggest obstacle you are facing right now Mr./Ms. Client? What is your current strategic plan to solve these issues?

HOW: How is it working, any issues?

WHY: Why do you think you are having these issues?

WHO: Who are you currently working with to solve these issues? How is that going?

WHEN: When do you think you will overcome these issues?

WHERE: Where do you see yourself in 6 months, 12months and 24 months?

Back to WHAT: what are doing to reach these goals? You go on and on till you pinpoint the issues your client is facing and how & what can you add to the mix to solve these issues.

Tried and True – Make a difference in someone's life today,

Teresa Cloninger

More than once I have worked hard on selling to a customer without finding out their capabilities, or lack thereof, to pay for the product. I was busy selling when I should have been gathering information from the customer.

I have also sold hard to someone and found out, after everything was said and done, that I was talking to someone who could not make the buying decision. I should have been talking to their boss.

So there are lots of reasons to ask a lot of questions and be a good listener. Also, take notes. It is hard to remember everything said in a meeting but this also makes the customer feel that his words are important to you.

Crocker Smith

4. What percent of sales are lost in the first 60 seconds?

We are entering a time of "information overload". Every one of our customers are exposed to a minimum of one thousand advertising messages every day. In addition to being interrupted every eight minutes with some type of problem, phone call or employee, they are being called on by hundreds of sales people. Not only by our direct competitors, but also from the local radio station, the local TV station, the news paper, the girl scouts and boy scouts, the baseball and football team, the chamber of commerce, the restaurant association, the insurance company, the health inspector, job applicants, the list goes on and on. Is it any wonder that when we walk in or call our customer their attitude is one of defense? If we call on them once a week there are hundreds of things that have taken place since our last call.

To get a customer to listen there is one of two things we can do. We can fall in with their attitude, or we can change it. From there on our job is easy. For the moment, we are going to examine this principle and apply it to our job of selling. We are going to apply it to only one phase of that selling process, namely the first moment we spend in the presence of the prospect. And I do not think I exaggerate when I say that ninety percent of the sales we lose are mishandled in the first crucial moment.

What can we do or say to make our sales call more effective? Every time we call on one of our accounts to present a new product or service, or even to simply get an order, there is a preliminary process we must go through or we will loose before we even begin. We must have their full attention.

Once the small talk is over you must have an attention getter. When you shift gears and start to sell you run headlong into the first attitude of the prospect, an attitude which is impossible to influence until you understand it. The first step in your sale is to sell an attitude of receptivity. Remember your objective is to get him to say, "all right. I am interested. I want to hear your complete story!" Blot everything else out of your mind except attaining this first objective. If you don't swing his or her attitude you can talk for five hours to no effect. To under-estimate the value of this first crucial moment is the common fault of most sales people.

We have to say something or show the customer something that will peak their interest in such a way that will make them forget all the things that are currently occupying their mind. What can we do or say that will accomplish this important step in the sale; getting attention? Here are a few of the old standby's that work every time:

Ask for advice. When done in a sincere way this is an excellent way to compliment someone and get their attention at the same time. "We brought in a new product and would like to ask your advice on how it might be sold".

A piece of industry news. When you come across a news story that may have an effect on your customer's business, cut it out, make a copy for everyone you are going to call on during the week, write their name on, and use it as an attention getter. Caution. Whenever you hand someone something to read, do not talk until they finish reading. If you start talking they will become confused. "Do you want me to listen or do you want me to read?" They will end up doing neither.

Hand them a sales brochure, be silent, and wait for them to respond. There are thousands of dollars worth of Point Of Sale material in every sales office that goes unused. POS material is an excellent tool to get a persons attention. A big mistake is to give in to the overwhelming urge to talk while the customer is reading. Give the customer the sales brochure and be silent. Soon the customer will make a comment or ask a question. At that point you have succeeded in getting their attention.

Try an experiment the next time you call on a customer. Take a manila folder and write the persons name on the tab large enough so it can be easily read from across the desk. Put everything in the file you want to talk about and watch the reaction when you pull the file out and lay it on the table. The message you are sending is that you think this person is important enough to have a special file and you took the time to put together the items you wanted to talk about.

Another approach is to take your monthly sales brochure and highlight the items each particular customer buys from you. This extra time will double the power of your fliers. Write their name on the POS before you go into the presentation and watch the difference.

Another example is the use of samples. When a sample is given to a customer we have the urge to tell them everything about it. The longer you can remain silent the more attention the customer will give to the sample. They have to be given a chance to look it over, taste it, feel it and smell it. We know so much about the product that we want to talk about it. Relax and give the customer some room to get involved with the sample. When it is time to talk - the customer will let you know.

Just about everyone in this country is in debt and just about everyone feels the responsibility to pay their debts. We can duplicate a strategy used for several years by a company that sold household products door to door. Their strategy was to knock on the door and when the homemaker answered, the sales person would present them with a small gift. Because of our feeling of obligation to repay our debts, the prospect would listen to the sales presentation. The same feeling of obligation lies within every person we deal with. They may or may not repay the debt, nevertheless, they feel the obligation. The next time you make a cold call on a prospect, take along a small gift and present it at the beginning of the interview. It can be as simple as a company calendar, an ink pen or a note pad. Nine out of ten times they will repay you by listening to your presentation.

Product cost, labor cost, increasing customer base, increasing check size, new ideas to help build business, marketing and merchandising ideas, new products or services, success stories, their profit and loss statement, all are good for getting attention.

A completed sale is only the SUM OF A NUMBER OF SEPARATE SALES... each a sale in itself ... each step in the sale should be thought of and handled alone ... and the sum of all the separate sales is greater than each part. Again I repeat, treat the first step, the opener, as a sale.

Concentrate on the prospect's original attitude. Change it! Then go on with the presentation . . . with the door wide open.

Comments:

Having an attention getter such as a special sheet or a WOW item to show your client helps generate sales. Often, all you have to do is hand it to them and let them look at it and ask any questions they might have and then write up the sale.

Phil Hackett

This section brings up an excellent point that we often don't think of. Nobody can read and listen at the same time. This is another one of those times where we need to practice being quiet, and as painful as it may seem, it works! I used it the last time I approached someone in a casual conversation about job opportunities with this company. I was asked for my resume, and when I handed it to her, I noticed that she actually looked down at it and started to read it. I fought the urge to begin talking about my skills and qualifications. Instead, I waited silently until she raised her head and looked at me. Then SHE started asking questions. To make a long story short, he hired me two weeks later! So I feel as my silence played a major part in not overwhelming the manager with my accomplishments, education, etc… She was able to review my information, ask the questions she wanted answers to, in turn SHE was in control of the interview.

Brooke Knight

Bob, I would say "information overload" is the UNDERSTATEMENT of the millennium. In today's high tech world is you can't multi task and do eight things at once you are thought of as lazy and left in the dust! You MUST be creative, think outside of the box to grab your clients attention

Yes, Yes, Yes………..

Sales Collateral- also called POS (point of sale) material. If you are mailing this to a client- make the package heavy (put a gift into it). I once mailed my customers rocks. Yes- I said rocks- You had to be there- the imagery used on the POS material was a solid foundation (IE rocks). Another idea I used was to hand address the clients name and address with lots of swirls and hearts on the envelope and dabbed on some perfume. I just put our mailing address on the back of the envelope- Not our name. Both of these evoked a TON of response.

Folder with Client Name: I too have used this technique- IT WORKS. I put all the research about the company, their needs, their competition, etc in the file. It was over an inch think. The Client later told us one of the reasons we got the bid was because of how prepared we were. We did not just tell them – We showed them!

Gifts: You have to be a little careful on this one. It has almost become a given- Don't let your customer see you as a big, walking credit card!

I like to "give" information. Like the news items, what's working in other areas, useful information that does not even deal with my product. This helps set you apart to become more of a consultant. When you speak- everyone listens.

Asking for their advice or thoughts on a topic is ALWAYS helpful.

The list could go on and on. The point to remember is set yourself apart from the background noise of everyday life.

Out of the box thinker (or just off my rocker)-you decide,

Teresa Cloninger

5. What is the easiest way to overcome objections?

Anyone who will not complain about price is not very interested in what we are selling.

When the average person thinks seriously about buying some article or service that costs real money, they think at once also of reasons for not buying it. This is true even if they have the desire to buy and have practically made up their mind to buy.

To understand objections and why they are raised, just look at yourself: Suppose you have been getting along in your tiny 3 bedroom home, and suppose your earnings are good and you have the money to buy a better house. Then suppose a real estate friend calls, tells you about this great house that just came on the market.

You say to yourself, "I really don't need a new house. I'm getting along all right with the old one. It's foolish to spend this money right now - I might need it for something else.... On the other hand, my house needs a new roof and some other repairs. It may not be safe....Then again, why should I buy THIS house? I saw one Sunday and it looked pretty good to me ... Of course, I want to stay in the neighborhood ... still, that house was mighty nice. Then there's the new addition on the other side of town.... I wonder what my wife/husband will think about buying a new house? He or she is not so hot about spending money.

You can see how easy it is to come up with at least 5 objections before we get serious about making the purchase.

Always keep in mind that the buyer is comfortable dealing with the sales person and company they are buying from. To make a change requires assurances that you will be able to handle their business.

In the buyers mind it is easier to stay with their current supplier even if the prices and delivery are not exactly as they would like. That is why they have at least five objections that we must overcome before a prospect will feel sure enough to give us their business.

The point is you should always be prepared for the objections you know will come up. If you ever watch how a comedian works an intoxicated audience and overcomes the wise cracks they throw at the speaker you have to wonder how they are able to respond so quickly. Here is there secret. Every comment and wise crack has been anticipated. They practice and practice until their response sounds like it was thought up on the spot. We should do the same homework with the anticipated objections we KNOW always come up.

Here are the top 27 objections you will most likely run up against:

1. What makes you any different form my current supplier

2. I really don't think much of your company

3. We've been doing all right without you

4. I'm tied up in a supplier contract

5. You don't carry the items I need

6. I'm not interested in anything new

7. See me in a couple of months

8. I hear your company is having problems

9. I am not talking to anyone right now - business is down

10. Your prices have always been too high

11. $40 a case! You have to do better than that

12. I have to run that by the owner

13. If I pay that much - what will you do for me

14. I have to have monthly terms to buy from you.

15. I don't care about anything but price

16. I want a volume discount on this order

17. I am SHOCKED at how high your price is

18. I'm paying $10 - your price is $12 why should I buy yours

19. Your competitor is a lot cheaper than you are

20. It would be too much work to change suppliers

21. Can I have a discount on the first order

22. If I use you, I have to have a 6:00 am delivery

23. I don't want to jeopardize the supplier relationship we have

24. If I changed suppliers why would I be any better off

25. I'm too busy to talk to you right now

26. I'm buying from a friend

27. I tried your company once and you screwed up the order

Comments:

Another reason the buyer doesn't want to pursue or entertain your proposal/pitch is that they subconsciously but immediately perceive evaluating you as a new supplier as more WORK! They are comfortable in their current routine/arrangement and now you are suggesting they do some extra work to see about possible CHANGE?

Doug Barringer

There are two types of objections that I usually experience: The standard, "I am not going to waste my time with you because I don't need your product" and "I need your product but there are some reasons that are keeping me from buying from you". I believe the first category is tougher to overcome because you have to start from scratch and spark some interest from the potential customer which can be very difficult with the usual time constraints involved.

If the customer already has interest, they are a qualified buyer and you can begin the process of making the purchase easy for them by answering their objections individually. You have gone from "why would I buy this product?" to 'why wouldn't I buy this product?". This is a very methodical process.

Crocker Smith

Objections are just our customer's way of saying "I may be interested in what this person has to offer". We in response should LISTEN CAREFULLY to what they are saying, suggesting, or whatever it is that they need to help them to overcome what they are really concerned about in their buying. Then, our job is to help overcome their doubts about buying by presenting the advantages. When the customer feels that we have listened to them, have been understanding of what their concerns are and ease those fears by sensibly presenting the ways they are going to benefit; then we have helped them to make the best decision logically and we both have won in the end. And, as salespeople we learn to carry that experience on in a future similar situation involving the same objection. We learn from every objection experience how to handle the situation better in the future. Practice makes perfect!

Brooke Knight

An objection can almost always be overcome if you can give the buyer just a few more reason to buy than they have already come up with on there own. Most people just need a bit of a nudge in the direction you want them to go. And with practice this will become a valuable and familiar tool in your sales tool box to which we should always be adding to and using.

Brian Spraggins

Objections are difficult at times because for so many when they hear an objection they think its rejection. An objection to me is the buyer asking me why my service is better than the one they are getting now. Its just one more way we can highlight what we do as to what everyone claims to do.

Brandon Sanchez

It's only second nature to over analyze everything we do. Even when we know we want to buy something and we have found the one that we want, for some reason we have to justify to ourselves buying it. We need to show them why their investment is going to be worth it.

Matthew Thacker

The good thing about objections is that you either overcome them or learn something from it when you don't overcome them. When your study the people you deal with and try to understand why the act the way they do will help you to figure out or learn how to handle them better the next time you come around them. I agree that every sales call you make is a learning opportunity into what makes sales people stronger.

Yessie Narvaez

Objections are natural and as you said expected. I am always faced with objections or questions. My goal is to anticipate the objections or questions and be ready with an answer that will satisfy the client. This is not always the case, unfortunately in sales there is no perfect guide to follow and every client will have different objections or questions. My philosophy is if at first you don't succeed try,

try again. Continue to be seen and even if they have gone to a competitor for now you want to be prepared for the moment that competitor slips up. Never accept defeat just wait and go back at a later time. Strength of character will shine through.

Kathie Luttrell

I wasn't thinking of buying a house until my agent friend called me and put the idea into my head, therefore I really don't need to purchase the house. Well from a buyers point of view about objections the cool headed response is to not purchase the house. When selling I don't want to make anyone buy into anything that is not a good deal and that is something they don't want!

Morgan Frazier

6. How many closing strategies do you need?

Some sales people believe that selling will become a dying trade with all the technology available today. However, just the opposite is true. With more and more products coming on the market every day there are an equal amount of choices to be made by the buyers. Without good sales people the customers will be lost when trying to make decisions without the help of an "assistant buyer". Marketing will never replace a sales person either. Marketing is merely finding a prospect with a need or desire for the product or service, selling is making the presentation and getting the order. Following are a couple of different ways to ask:

The direct close is one of the best ways to close because you get it over with up front and there is no doubt about what you are there for. We literally start the presentation with the close. Simply ask for what you want as you start your presentation and build your presentation on the anticipated objections. One thing that is extremely important in using this tactic is you have to know exactly what you want before making the call. An example: "I have done everything you required to earn your business, is there anything else standing in the way of us moving forward?".

The choice close is the most common close, however, it is often incorrectly used. If you wait until the end of the presentation and then try and squeeze the customer into a corner they will resent it. The correct way to use this tactic is to build it into your presentation by offering two or three different choices, explaining all the differences as well as the features and benefits of each product, and let them choose the one that best fits their needs. The theory behind this close is that you give them a choice between something you want and something else you want and let them make the choice. You never want to give them a choice between something and nothing.

This close is especially good for the "price buyer". You can show the low quality product, the middle quality product and the high quality product, pointing out that the higher price is really going to cost less in the long run.

The time advantage close creates a sense of urgency during the presentation. "While supply lasts" implies that there are several other sales people selling the same program and if you don't put your order in right now you might miss out. "Limited time only" implies that the price will soon go back to the book price. "Sale ends Friday" also creates the feeling of missing out on an opportunity. "One time offer" is designed to put pressure on to take advantage of the promotion now or miss out all together.

"Longer shelf life" is also a way of taking advantage of time if the shorter shelf life of a competitor is causing a loss due to waste. "New inventory is higher" implies that the market has gone up and you are holding your price down until you sell out of our current stock.

The ask again close must be used carefully otherwise it will be mistaken as high pressure. Wait a short period of time then ask again as if you were asking for the first time. The theory behind this close is the time it takes for a new idea or concept to take hold. It takes time for the mind to work and when you ask the first time there is a natural defense mechanism at work. However, after just a few minutes the buyers mind will start making mental associations and will have more information available to make the decision. It's similar to a computer making a "search".

It also takes courage to ask a second or third time. This extra effort is what makes a closer. Anybody can ask once and accept a negative response. A famous football coach was asked once how he was able to pick such good players for his team. His response was that he looks for players who make the "Extra effort". Everybody can play well or they wouldn't even be in the consideration stage, however, it's those special few who stretch a little further.

Three out of four sales people do not ask the prospect to buy after the sales presentation. The bottom line of being a good closer is to always know what you want before making the call, and then do what only one in four sales people do; never be shy about asking for it.

Comments:

The time advantage close was used to perfection by a local furniture store. First they would have a "Total Inventory Reduction Sale". Then a "Bankruptcy Liquidation Sale". And finally a "Selling Out To The Bare Walls Sale". Of course they never went out of business. They just kept cycling through these sales for several years. But it made you notice them and contemplate going in to see how good of a deal you could get.

Of course, professional sales people know that they would lose credibility if they tried anything like this.

But you have to try to give your product some exclusivity along with a slight sense of urgency in the customer's mind to facilitate the close.

Crocker Smith

It really doesn't matter what closing strategy you use, as long as it's working for you. I customize my closings based on each individual prospect. I like to get a "feel" for the person and their company, educate myself a little on "them". Of course sometimes that is not possible, so in those instances I would take a different approach. The closing is the utmost important factor of the presentation. If all we had to do is make presentations I would be a millionaire already. In actuality if we are not closing, our presentation obviously was not as great as we thought. That is something that you have to evaluate yourself on, find room for improvement. The #1 objective is to KNOW WHAT YOU WANT, AND ASK FOR IT!!! Continue to follow up with these people. It takes a few NO'S before you get a yes, so for every NO you hear it puts you that much closer to a YES!!!

Brooke Knight

Closing, as a whole, is probably the most important facet of a presentation. Although, unlike the other aspects of a presentation, your closing will greatly depend on your situation. You want to close strong, but not so strong that you come off as strong arming the meeting. That's why I believe the choice close is a powerful and effective close but should be used with understanding of how to set the choice up.

Matthew Thacker

The close has to be the hardest part. Closing takes a lot of tact. I like the idea of giving them some options to choose from and it appears that not purchasing anything is not an option. I look forward to tweaking my closing skills.

Morgan Frazier

I have always liked asking directly, "is there anything preventing you from making a decision today" – this makes clear any objections the customer may have so that you can address them as well as letting you know exactly where you stand with the customer and where they are in the decision making process.

Danielle Antonacci

"I had no idea the intricacies, involved in closing. The common close is one I use a lot but the others, rarely if ever. I could use a little help with the direct close, I don't recall ever using it and I don't quite understand how to work it into a presentation. I guess I could use some suggestions."

Shannon Smith

Here are two examples:

"Bill, I have given you all the information and pricing you requested - is this a good time to put together your first order?"

"Joe, how many cases of this new item do you want me to add to your order?"

7. What percent of sales people follow up?

Every now and then you will hear a sales manager enthusiastically talk about a new sales person.

"If I had ten people like him out in the field we could double our business - in the first two weeks he brought in one of the largest orders we've ever had!"

Whenever I hear stories like this I wonder how successful they will be six months down the road. In today's business the most profitable sales person is the one who "wears well". The sales person who can call on prospects, close sales, make recalls, close more sales, and each year build a greater volume of business from each customer with a greater amount of confidence and respect from the customer.

There are many sales people who can be sent over a territory once, but not twice. They make a good first impression, a good presentation, close the first order, and then they are off for the next challenge. They don't like to go back to the same customer twice and are usually not welcome because of the lack of follow up.

The majority of sales people follow up to some degree, but only 10% fall into the category that do it like a true professional.

The satisfaction that comes from doing one thing absolutely right and putting the trade-mark of your character on it, far outweighs the value of a thousand half done jobs. As a professional sales person, your follow up and attention to detail is your trade-mark.

The quality that you put into your work effects everything else in your life. Your entire personality takes on the characteristics of the way you do things. The habit of following up and taking care of the details not only strengthens your selling ability, but improves your whole personality.

On the other hand, doing things in a careless manner also effect every other part of your life. Every half-done job that goes out of your hands leaves its trace behind. After slighting your work, after doing a poor job, you are not quite the same person you were before. You are not so likely to try and keep up the standard of your work.

The moral effect of carelessly doing things has the power to drag you down. You cannot respect yourself if you habitually leave dozens of things undone. When self-respect drops, confidence goes with it, and when confidence and self-respect have gone, excellence in your selling skills is impossible.

Your work habits need constant watching in order to keep up your standards. This is even more important for you, a sales person, because most of your time is spent working alone. Many sales people let their ideals drop when they are not under constant supervision and suffer because of it.

There is an old saying that sums up the importance of good follow up: "The secret of success is to do the common job uncommonly well."

Comments:

I have always heard that the follow up was the hardest part of selling. Sometimes I can see where some people may feel that way, but the follow up is going to be based off of how well the initial call went. If you made a good first impression then obviously it will make the follow up much more enjoyable. Now if you went in unprepared and did not make a good impression then it may make a sales person not want to make that follow up. Regardless, following up is a part of selling, something everyone should take very seriously, and something you should not be shy about doing.

Jason Kirouac

Follow up to an initial visit or order is simple. At this point it takes no work, you have already gotten the order or the initial visits, all you have to do now is show up and say hi. When I talk to my clients and prospective clients I always tell them that I am not looking to fill one order for you but I want to develop a long term relationship where you will call me when you have a need. I want to be the go to person for their needs.

Brandon Sanchez

Follow up is the "holy grail" of sales, great to speak about but few that actively seek it. Following up after a sale or even after a presentation shows persistence. Even if you don't get the sale, following up could lead to future sales. If they buy from someone else and then just never hear from them again they may realize they should have gone with you in the first place. You never know what present no may turn into a future yes.

Matthew Thacker

The number one ingredient to become successful in sales is to keep in touch with people and build relationships. Everyone wants to feel special, remembered and valued. Sometimes our busy schedules leave little time to think about appreciate or thank anyone in our lives. Going the extra mile, which might only take an extra few minutes a day, to appreciate your clients and prospective clients is a must to reach your goals. Building relationships takes time, but it is well worth it at the end. Think of how nice it feels for you when you receive a follow-up call, email, note or card. The same is true for everyone else as well.

Yessenia Narvaez

If I say it once a day, I say it a million times, do it right the first time, don't take shortcuts in life or your life will be cut short. Following up shows that we care about our clients. Whether we take a box of donuts, or just stop in to say hi, it's very important to let them know that when we promised them that they would get "us", we meant it. The people who get the business, and don't follow up on the business, lose the business. It's just a matter of time.

Kimberly Burgess

Following up with clients, new and old is not a difficult task. Following up with prospects is more of a challenge. I feel like I pretty much know where I stand with my clients and I do everything in my power to make them feel important. A prospect is not as clearly defined. If I tell them I am going to do something I certainly follow through with it though.

Lisa Lloyd

My uncle once told me a salesperson came by his office and was ecstatic that a prospect said no for the fourth time in a row. The salesperson knew the fifth time he called the prospect, there was a high probability he would then get a chance to earn the business. I try to document every time I call a prospect and make the return phone calls when I say I will call. People will remember a consistent person and refer other friends to you for business.

Gregg Nixon

It seems so simple to say, but truer words have never been spoken. I like to think that I'm pretty thorough with my follow up, but deep down I know there is room for improvement. We can't afford to be lazy when it comes to this area.

Jonathan Kendig

To me, follow-up is the easiest part. I don't want my customers to feel like I just "sold" them anything – I want them to feel like we entered a relationship and the only way to do that is to keep in contact and follow-up. Lack of follow-up, in my opinion, makes the customer feel like they were just sold something, and now that the sale is complete their value has declined – when in reality the opposite should be true. The sale is just the beginning.

Danielle Antonacci

"Follow up is the key to the kingdom!!"

I completely agree with this statement. And I will admit that I am not perfect. But I see every current client I have at least once every week. I deliver payroll and I don't leave it with a secretary. I see the plant manager, the shift supervisor, the owner or whomever I possibly can. I want them to know that whether I have one employee with them or 50 they are important to me. I take gifts, ie….pens, tablets, candy, coffee, doughnuts or whatever I can to let them know they are #1.

Every client is #1 to me because they all make up my business and I don't want to loose a single one. Granted some will not need me for very long, but if they feel appreciated they will remember and when someone they know is looking for an employee they will recount what a good experience they had working with me and that is a pay off you can't afford to loose. I once read or heard that if someone has a negative experience they will tell about 20 people. When someone has a good experience they will tell about 5 people. I sincerely believe that.

So I have to make 4 people happy to get that 20 people to hear about a good experience. So I focus everyday on making at least 4 people happy. That works out to 100 people a week. Follow up is the key to the kingdom!!

Kathie Luttrell

A Financial Consultant of mine about 10 years ago told me something that I will never forget. He was over at my place to go over my (believe me) very small portfolio. He always had coffee, sat with me and discussed many things. This particular evening he was a little late because the previous client took a little longer - they were working on a large deal. It was no problem for me but I told him that he could have rescheduled the meeting; after all, my account was not very big. He told me the area that he came from and it is a very wealthy area of town. I assumed that it was a very lucrative deal so I asked him why he spends so much time with me.

His answer was that many sales reps go after the quick fix , the adrenaline high / rush of the sale of the moment and move on to the next challenge. They forget the follow up and as a result are always running after the big one because someone is eating up their business from behind due to lack of follow up. They last for maybe 2 years and move on, always running , always gaining in the short term and then running out of steam. My consultant figured that by ensuring solid follow up on all accounts he was building his future. And he did.

Jim Land

About the author Bob Oros

Regardless of whether you are reading one of his books or attending one of his programs, the most frequent comment is: "This guy has been there, he is one of us, I am going to use these strategies."

With over 2,000 speaking engagements in all 50 states and several international locations for manufacturers, distributors and associations, you can be sure you will get the results and information you are looking for. Prior to starting his speaking career, Bob served six years in the US Navy as a Communications Specialist and then worked his way from a street sales person to the position of National Sales Manager for a Fortune 200 company.

Bob has received awards for speaking, writing and marketing too numerous to mention.

Contents of the entire course

Why Sales People Fail

The Key to Selling Anybody

The Power of Expectations

Add Value to Every Product

Never Make the First Offer

How to Justify Your Price

Lost in 60 Seconds

One Good Reason to Buy

Control a Buyer's Attitude

How to Create Demand

Smoke Screen Objections

Take the Risk Out of Sales

How Small Companies Get Big

www.ingramcontent.com/pod-product-compliance
Lightning Source LLC
Chambersburg PA
CBHW021911170526
45157CB00005B/2046